Caleb's Year

_____

Name

EMC 6481 • © Evan-Moor Corp.

It is spring.
The days are windy and warm.

1

Baby birds learn to fly.
Caleb learns to fly—a kite!
He is six years old.

2

Summer days are long.
There is a lot of time to play.

3

Butterflies play in the flowers.
Caleb plays ball with his friends.

4

It is fall.
Leaves are yellow, orange, red, and brown.

5

Squirrels are at work.
Caleb does his work in school.

6

Winter is here. It is cold.
Snow falls all around.

7

Animals make tracks in the snow.
Caleb makes tracks, too.

8

The seasons come and go.
First comes spring, then summer, fall, and winter.
And now, Caleb is seven.

9

Dictionary

Look at the picture. Read the word.
Write the word on the line.

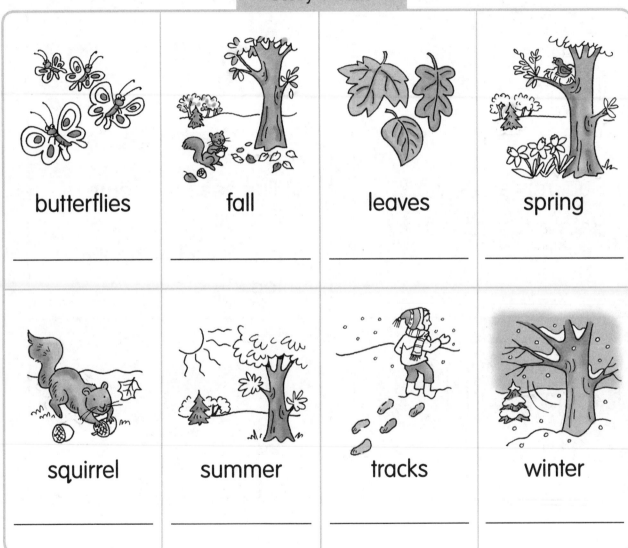

Story Words

butterflies

fall

leaves

spring

_____

_____

_____

_____

squirrel

summer

tracks

winter

_____

_____

_____

_____

Words to Know

around	cold	flowers
learn	seasons	warm
windy	work	year

I Read Closely

Read. Mark the sentence that goes with the picture.

- ○ Squirrels are at work.
- ○ Baby birds learn to fly.

- ○ The seasons come and go.
- ○ Caleb makes tracks, too.

- ○ Caleb does his work in school.
- ○ Animals make tracks in the snow.

- ○ And now, Caleb is seven.
- ○ Summer days are long.

I Read and Understand

Read and answer.

1. In the spring, Caleb learns to fly a ____.
   - ○ kite
   - ○ bird

2. In the summer, Caleb plays ____ with his friends.
   - ○ school
   - ○ ball

3. In the fall, Caleb goes to ____.
   - ○ snow
   - ○ school

4. In the winter, Caleb makes ____.
   - ○ tracks
   - ○ leaves

5. At the end of the story, Caleb is ____.
   - ○ seasons
   - ○ seven

I Tell the Story

Finish the pictures. Tell someone the story.

1 Draw the kite.

2 Draw the ball.

3 Draw Caleb.

4 Draw the tracks.

I told the story to _____.

I Read Realistic Fiction

Realistic fiction is a made-up story.
But the author makes it seem like real life.
In "Caleb's Year" the author has Caleb grow older.

Time Order

1. We know that time passes in the story because _____.

   ○ Caleb is a boy

   ○ the seasons come and go

2. One year passes in the story. Write the seasons that go by. Put them in order.

   _____   _____

   _____   _____

Beginning, Middle, End

3. What happens at the beginning of the story?

   ○ Caleb is six years old.

   ○ Caleb makes tracks in the snow.

4. What happens at the end of the story?

   ○ Caleb plays ball with his friends.

   ○ Caleb is seven years old.

I Can Write

Write the words to finish each sentence.

Word Box

are long	fall, and winter
come and go	cold

1. The seasons _____.

2. Summer days _____.

3. Winter is _____.

4. First comes spring, then summer, _____

   _____.

Write your own sentence. Tell about one of the seasons.

5. _____

   _____

   _____

   _____

Color

A Poem by Christina Rossetti

_____

_____
Name

EMC 6481 • © Evan-Moor Corp.

What is pink? A rose is pink
By a fountain's brink.

What is red? A poppy's red
In its barley bed.

2

What is blue? The sky is blue
Where the clouds float through.

3

What is white? A swan is white
Sailing in the light.

4

What is yellow? Pears are yellow,
Rich and ripe and mellow.

5

EMC 6481 • © Evan-Moor Corp.

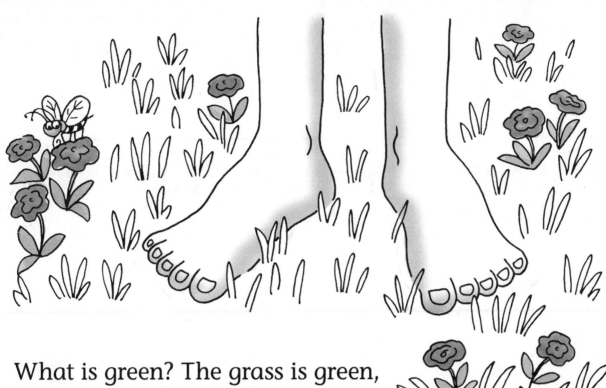

What is green? The grass is green,
With small flowers between.

6

EMC 6481 • © Evan-Moor Corp.

What is violet? Clouds are violet
In the summer twilight.

7

What is orange? Why, an orange,
Just an orange!

8

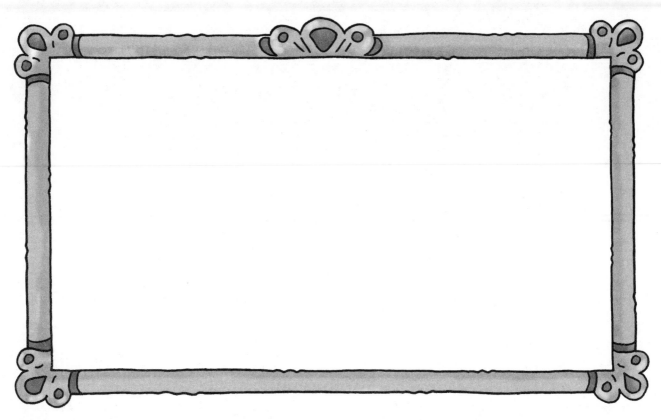

Draw a garden full of color.

9

Dictionary

Look at the picture. Read the word.
Write the word on the line.

Story Words

barley

fountain

light

pears

_____

_____

_____

_____

poppy

rose

sailing

swan

_____

_____

_____

_____

Words to Know

between	brink	clouds
float	mellow	rich
ripe	twilight	violet

I Read Closely

Read. Mark the sentence that goes with the picture. Then color.

○ What is yellow?

○ What is orange?

○ What is pink?

○ What is red?

○ What is violet?

○ What is white?

○ What is blue?

○ What is orange?

I Read and Understand

Read and answer.

1. The name of the poem is ____.
   - ○ Pink
   - ○ Color

2. A rose is pink by a fountain's ____.
   - ○ brink
   - ○ cloud

3. The ____ is blue where the clouds float through.
   - ○ swan
   - ○ sky

4. Clouds are violet in the summer ____.
   - ○ barley
   - ○ twilight

5. What is orange? Just an ____!
   - ○ orange
   - ○ pears

I Remember the Poem

Finish the sentences. Tell someone the poem.

 A rose is _____.

 A poppy is _____.

 The sky is _____.

 A swan is _____.

 Pears are _____.

 The grass is _____.

 Clouds are _____.

 An orange is _____.

I told the poem to _____.

Word Box

violet

yellow

white

green

red

pink

orange

blue

Reading Literary Text • EMC 6481 • © Evan-Moor Corp.

I Read a Poem

A poem is a group of words
that tell about an idea or a feeling.
Poems may have a pattern.
Poems may have rhyme.

Idea

1. The poem tells about _____.

   ○ many colors
   ○ one color

Words That Rhyme

2. Read the sentence. Circle two words that rhyme.

   A swan is white sailing in the light.

Words, Words, Words

3. Write the missing words in the pattern.

   What is green? The _____ is green.

   What is white? A _____ is white.

   What is yellow? _____ are yellow.

I Can Write

Write the words to finish each line of the poem.

Word Box

its barley bed   fountain's brink

rose is pink   poppy's red

1. What is pink? A _____

2. By a _____.

3. What is red? A _____

4. In _____.

Write your own sentence. Use a color word and a rhyming word.

5. _____

_____

_____

Bed in Summer
A Poem by Robert Louis Stevenson

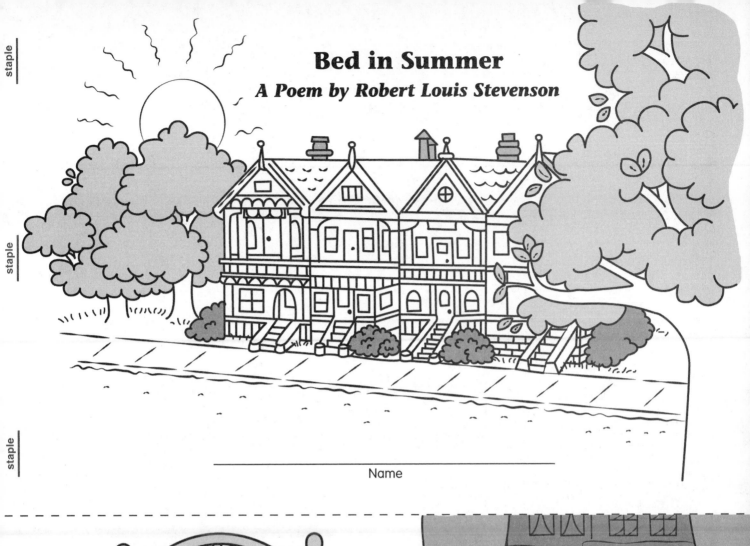

Name _____

In winter I get up at night
And dress by yellow candle-light.

EMC 6481 • © Evan-Moor Corp.

1

In summer, quite the other way,
I have to go to bed by day.

2

I have to go to bed and see
The birds still hopping on the tree,

3

Or hear the grown-up people's feet
Still going past me in the street.

4

And does it not seem hard to you,
When all the sky is clear and blue,

5

EMC 6481 • © Evan-Moor Corp.

And I should like so much to play,
To have to go to bed by day?

EMC 6481 • © Evan-Moor Corp.

Draw your own dream.

8

Robert Louis Stevenson
was a famous writer.
He wrote books and poems.
He was often sick when
he was a boy.
Little Robert had to stay in bed.
But he loved to read stories.

9

Dictionary

Look at the picture. Read the word.
Write the word on the line.

Story Words

birds

_____

candle-light

_____

dream

_____

feet

_____

night

_____

street

_____

writer

_____

Words to Know

clear	grown-up	hard
hear	hopping	much
other	quite	should

I Read Closely

....

Read. Mark the words that go with the picture.

○ The birds still hopping on the tree,

○ And I should like so much to play,

○ In winter I get up at night

○ Or hear the grown-up people's feet

○ And dress by yellow candle-light.

○ When all the sky is clear and blue,

○ I have to go to bed by day.

○ And I should like so much to play,

I Read and Understand

Read and answer.

1. "Bed in Summer" is a ____.
   - ○ story
   - ○ poem

2. The ____ speaks in the poem.
   - ○ mother
   - ○ boy

3. In ____ the boy gets up at night.
   - ○ birds
   - ○ winter

4. In ____ the boy goes to bed by day.
   - ○ summer
   - ○ quite

5. Robert Louis Stevenson loved to ____.
   - ○ hear
   - ○ read

I Tell the Story

Finish the pictures. Tell someone the story.

1 Draw the candle.

2 Draw the sun.

3 Draw the tree.

4 Draw the face.

I told the story to _____.

I Read a Poem

A poem is a group of words that tell about
an idea, a feeling, or something that happened.
Some poems have a beat.
Some poems have rhyme.

Idea

1. One idea from this poem is ____.

   ○ the boy feels sleepy on a summer night

   ○ the boy wants to stay up and play

Words That Rhyme

2. Circle two words that rhyme.

   In summer, quite the other way,

   I have to go to bed by day.

Robert Louis Stevenson

3. Mark the things you read about the author of the poem.

   ○ He wrote books and poems.

   ○ He was famous.

   ○ He liked to draw pictures.

   ○ As a boy, he loved to read.

I Can Write

Write the words to finish each sentence.

Word Box

candle-light   bed by day

at night   the other way

1. In winter I get up _____

2. And dress by yellow _____.

3. In summer, quite _____,

4. I have to go to _____.

Write your own sentence. Tell something about summer or winter.

5. _____

_____

_____

_____

The Ant's Voice
A Tale from East Africa

Name

EMC 6481 • © Evan-Moor Corp.

Once upon a time an ant needed a new house.
The ant saw a cave. No one was home.
The ant crawled into the cave.

A lizard came home to the cave.
The lizard saw tracks.
"Who is in my house?" she called.

2

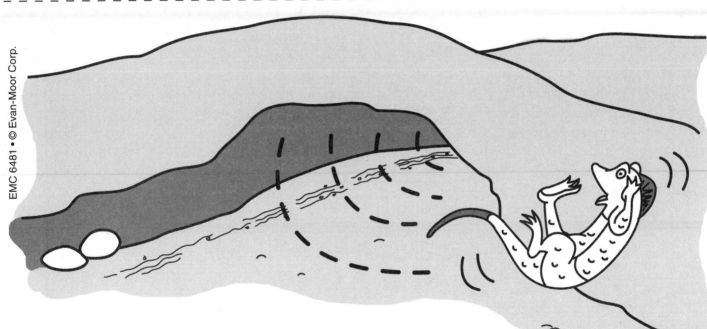

The ant's voice boomed from the cave.
"It is I! I am strong enough to crush an elephant.
Who dares to ask?"
The lizard ran away.

3

The lizard asked a warthog for help.
The warthog stood outside the cave.
"Who is in my friend's house?" he barked.

4

The ant's voice boomed from the cave.
"It is I! I am strong enough to crush an elephant.
Who dares to ask?"
The warthog ran away.

5

The lizard asked a tiger for help.
The tiger stood outside the cave.
"Who is in my friend's house?" she growled.

6

The ant's voice boomed from the cave.
"It is I! I am strong enough to crush an elephant.
Who dares to ask?"
The tiger jumped back.

7

The lizard asked a little frog for help.
The frog stood in the cave opening.
"I am strong enough to crush anyone who can crush
an elephant!" croaked the frog in a big voice.

8

The ant shook when he saw the frog's big shadow.
"I have had my fun," said the ant.
And the ant ran right out of the cave!

9

Dictionary

Look at the picture. Read the word.
Write the word on the line.

Story Words

ant

elephant

frog

lizard

_____

_____

_____

_____

shadow

tiger

voice

warthog

_____

_____

_____

_____

Words to Know

barked	boomed	crawled
croaked	crush	dares
growled	opening	strong

I Read Closely

Read. Mark the sentence that goes with the picture.

- ○ The warthog stood outside the cave.
- ○ The lizard ran away.

- ○ The tiger jumped back.
- ○ The ant crawled into the cave.

- ○ The lizard asked a little frog for help.
- ○ "Who is in my friend's house?" she growled.

- ○ "I have had my fun," said the ant.
- ○ The ant's voice boomed from the cave.

I Read and Understand

Read and answer.

1. The story of the ant's voice is ____.

   ○ true

   ○ made up

2. The animals in the story ____.

   ○ talk

   ○ sing

3. The ____ fooled the other animals.

   ○ lizard

   ○ ant

4. The ____ fooled the ant.

   ○ frog

   ○ elephant

5. The ____ made the ant's voice big.

   ○ cave

   ○ shadow

61

I Tell the Story

Finish the pictures. Tell someone the story.

1 Draw the ant going in.

2 Draw the cave.

3 Write the missing word.

Who dares to _____?

4 Draw the ant going out.

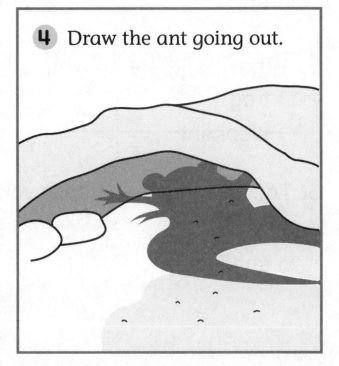

I told the story to _____.

I Read a Folk Tale

A folk tale is a made-up story.
Sometimes the characters are animals.
The characters can be good or bad.

Main Idea

1. What happened at the end of the story?

   ○ The lizard saw that she had been afraid of an ant.

   ○ The animals did not believe the lizard.

Animal Characters

2. List the characters.

   _____   _____

   _____   _____

   _____

Problem

3. What problem did the lizard have?

   ○ She was lost in a cave.

   ○ She wanted her house back.

4. Who took care of the problem?

   ○ the lizard   ○ the frog

I Can Write

Write the words to finish each sentence.

Word Box

from the cave   she called

and saw tracks   ran away

1. The lizard came home _____.

2. "Who is in my house?" _____.

3. The ant's voice boomed _____.

4. The lizard _____.

Write your own sentences. Tell about one animal in the story.

5. _____

_____

_____

_____

The Bear and the Bees

Aesop's Fable

Name

A bear went into the woods one day.
He was looking for things to eat.

1

The bear saw a log.
He smelled honey!

The bear nosed around the log.
"The bees are not home," he said to himself.

Just then a bee flew home from work.
She had been in the clover.

4

The bee saw the bear.
"I know what you want," buzzed the bee.

5

The bee flew at the bear and stung him.
Then the bee flew into the log.

6

"Ouch!" said the angry bear.
He used tooth and claw to get the nest.
Then all of the bees flew out.

7

The bear had to run to get away.
He had to jump in the pond to save himself!

8

Lesson: *It is wiser to put up with one hurt than to get angry and cause a thousand.*

9

Dictionary

Look at the picture. Read the word.
Write the word on the line.

Story Words

angry	bear	claw	clover
_____	_____	_____	_____
flew	honey	stung	woods
_____	_____	_____	_____

Words to Know

around	buzzed	himself	nosed
pond	save	smelled	things
thousand	tooth	used	work

I Read Closely

Read. Mark the sentence that goes with the picture.

○ The bear saw a log.

○ He had to jump in the pond to save himself!

○ "Ouch!" said the angry bear.

○ He was looking for things to eat.

○ He smelled honey!

○ "I know what you want," buzzed the bee.

○ She had been in the clover.

○ The bee flew at the bear and stung him.

I Read and Understand

Read and answer.

1. The story of the bear and the bees is ＿＿.

   ○ true

   ○ made up

2. The bees got angry when the bear ＿＿.

   ○ wanted honey

   ○ wanted to swim

3. The bee stung the bear to ＿＿.

   ○ make a new friend

   ○ make him go away

4. The bear jumped in the pond to ＿＿.

   ○ save himself

   ○ get the honey

5. The bear learned that it is not wise to ＿＿.

   ○ get angry

   ○ jump in the water

I Tell the Story

Finish the pictures. Tell someone the story.

1 Draw the log.

2 Trace the word.

3 Draw the bees.

4 Draw the pond.

I told the story to _____.

I Read a Fable

A fable is an old, old story.
The characters may be animals.
Sometimes the animals act like people.
A fable has a lesson.

Lesson

1. The bear learned that ____.

   ○ bears should not eat bees

   ○ getting angry makes things worse

Characters

2. Who are the story characters?

   _____   _____

3. Who got angry at the bees? _____

4. Who got angry at the bear? _____

Cause and Effect

5. Mark the things that happened because the bear got angry.

   ○ The bear had to jump in the pond to save himself.

   ○ The bear got the honey.

   ○ All the bees flew at the bear.

   ○ The bear went into the woods.

I Can Write

Write the words to finish each sentence.

Word Box

the angry bear   stung the bear

run away   to get the nest

1. The bee _____.

2. "Ouch!" said _____.

3. The angry bear wanted _____.

4. The bear had to _____.

Write your own sentence. Tell what the bear learned.

5. _____

_____

_____

_____

Three Little Kittens

by Mother Goose

Name _____

Three little kittens, they lost their mittens,
And they began to cry,
"Oh, mother dear, we sadly fear
Our mittens we have lost."

EMC 6481 • © Evan-Moor Corp.

1

"What! lost your mittens, you naughty kittens!
Then you shall have no pie."
"Meow, meow, meow."
"No, you shall have no pie."

The three little kittens, they found their mittens,
And they began to cry,
"Oh, mother dear, see here, see here,
Our mittens we have found!"

"Put on your mittens, you silly kittens,
And you shall have some pie."
"Purr, purr, purr,
Oh, let us have some pie."

4

The three little kittens put on their mittens,
And soon ate up the pie.
"Oh, mother dear, we greatly fear
Our mittens we have soiled."

5

"What! soiled your mittens, you naughty kittens!"
Then they began to sigh,
"Meow, meow, meow."
Then they began to sigh.

6

The three little kittens, they washed their mittens,
And hung them out to dry.
"Oh, mother dear, do you not hear,
Our mittens we have washed!"

7

"What! washed your mittens, then you're good kittens,
But I smell a rat close by."
"Meow, meow, meow.
We smell a rat close by."

8

THE END

9

Dictionary

Look at the picture. Read the word.
Write the word on the line.

Story Words

hear

_____

kittens

_____

mittens

_____

naughty

_____

pie

_____

silly

_____

soiled

_____

washed

_____

Words to Know

cry	dear	fear	found
greatly	hung	lost	meow
sadly	shall	sigh	

I Read Closely

Read. Mark the sentence that goes with the picture.

○ "Then you shall have no pie."

○ The three little kittens, they washed their mittens.

○ "Our mittens we have lost."

○ "Oh, let us have some pie."

○ Three little kittens, they lost their mittens.

○ "Our mittens we have washed!"

○ "Purr, purr, purr."

○ "We smell a rat close by."

I Read and Understand

Read and answer.

1. The three little kittens ____ their mittens.
   - ○ lost
   - ○ made

2. The kittens can have no ____.
   - ○ dry
   - ○ pie

3. The kittens ____ when they are happy.
   - ○ purr
   - ○ fear

4. The kittens ____ their soiled mittens.
   - ○ washed
   - ○ found

5. The kittens smell a ____.
   - ○ pie
   - ○ rat

I Tell the Story

Finish the pictures. Tell someone the story.

1 Draw the pie.

2 Draw the found mittens.

3 Draw the soiled mittens.

4 Draw the washtub.

I told the story to _____.

I Read a Nursery Rhyme

Nursery rhymes are fun to say.
They are very old. Some tell a story.
People say Mother Goose wrote them.
But she is a made-up person.

Story

1. The story was about ＿＿＿.

   ○ Mother Goose

   ○ kittens and mittens

Words That Rhyme

2. Circle two words that rhyme.

   Oh, mother dear, we sadly fear

Words for Sounds: Onomatopoeia

3. Some words name a sound. Circle two kitten sounds.

   meow   silly   purr

Word Opposites

4. Circle the words that are **opposites**.

   silly   lost   found

5. Circle the words that are **opposites**.

   naughty   cry   good

I Can Write

Write the words to finish each sentence.

Word Box

close by	we have found
have some pie	silly kittens

1. Our mittens _____!

2. Put on your mittens, you _____.

3. Oh, let us _____.

4. We smell a rat _____.

Write your own sentence. Tell about something the kittens did.

5. _____

_____

_____

_____

Mary's Fourth of July

_____

Name

EMC 6481 • © Evan-Moor Corp.

The Fourth of July is coming!
I am going to walk in the parade.
But these old shoes are tight.

1

A shoemaker came to our farm.
He measured my feet.
He will make my new shoes.

2

The Fourth of July will be fun.
Everyone goes to town.
My best friend Emily will be there.

3

Emily's mother measured and cut some cloth.
She is making a new dress.
Emily will have it for the parade.

4

It is Thursday.
My new shoes are here!
I have room to wiggle my toes.

5

Emily has a new dress.
I have new shoes.
We are ready for the Fourth of July parade.

6

It is Friday, the Fourth of July!
Emily and I walk in the parade.
Later, there are games and prizes.

7

My new shoes are lucky.
I won the sack race.

The prize was one silver dollar!

Dictionary

Look at the picture. Read the word.
Write the word on the line.

Story Words

cloth

_____

farm

_____

Fourth of July

_____

parade

_____

sack

_____

shoemaker

_____

shoes

_____

silver dollar

_____

Words to Know

best	everyone	friend	goes
lucky	making	measured	prize
race	tight	toes	wiggle

I Read Closely

Read. Mark the sentence that goes with the picture.

- ○ I have room to wiggle my toes.
- ○ But these old shoes are tight.

- ○ I won the sack race.
- ○ Emily has a new dress.

- ○ She is making a new dress.
- ○ My new shoes are lucky.

- ○ Everyone goes to town.
- ○ Emily and I walk in the parade.

I Read and Understand

Read and answer.

1. The story takes place ____.
   ○ today
   ○ long ago

2. Everyone goes to town for the ____.
   ○ Fourth of July
   ○ new shoes

3. Mary has new shoes for the ____.
   ○ farm
   ○ parade

4. Her new shoes are ____.
   ○ lucky
   ○ tight

5. The prize is a ____.
   ○ silver dollar
   ○ dress

I Tell the Story

Finish the pictures. Tell someone the story.

1 Draw the old shoes.

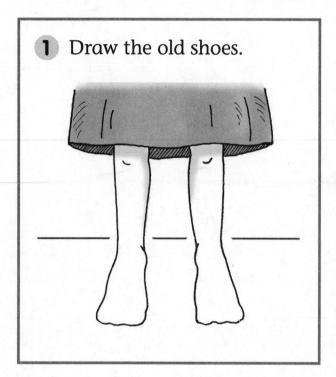

2 Draw the dots.

3 Draw the flags.

4 Draw the prize.

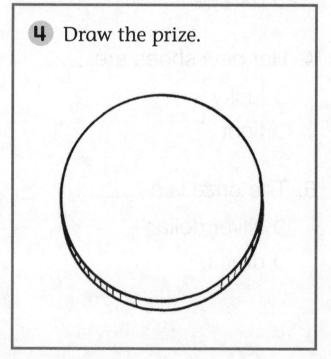

I told the story to _____.

I Read Historical Fiction

A fiction story is a made-up story.
The people, places, and happenings
in the story are make-believe.

Speaker

1. Who tells the story?

   ○ a shoemaker

   ○ Mary

2. How do you know the story is set in the past?

   ○ A shoemaker makes Mary's shoes.

   ○ Mary gets shoes at a store.

Problem

3. Mary's problem was _____.

   ○ she did not like parades

   ○ she needed new shoes

Cause and Effect

4. Mark the things that happened because Mary got new shoes.

   ○ She walked in the parade.   ○ She was sad.

   ○ She made a new dress.   ○ She had fun.

   ○ She wiggled her toes.   ○ She won a prize.

I Can Write

Write the words to finish each sentence.

Word Box

| wiggle my toes | to our farm |
| the sack race | are here |

1. A shoemaker came _____.

2. My new shoes _____!

3. I have room to _____.

4. I won _____.

Write your own sentence. Tell why Mary needed new shoes.

5. _____

_____

_____

Spider Woman
A Navajo Folk Tale

_____
Name

Spider Rock is a tall, tall rock in a canyon.
The people who live by the rock tell this story.

Long ago, Spider Woman helped the people.
She showed them how to make beautiful cloth.
Then she made her home at the top of Spider Rock.

2

One day, there was a peaceful young man.
He was being chased by an enemy.
He ran into the canyon to get away.

3

The young man looked up and saw Spider Rock.
He wanted to climb the tall rock.
"The rock is too tall," he said to himself.

4

Then he saw a thread. It was like magic.
The thread was hanging down from the tall rock.

5

The young man took hold of the magic thread.
He tied it around himself.
He climbed up to the top of Spider Rock.

6

The young man took a rest in that beautiful place.
When he looked down, his enemy was gone.

7

The young man turned around and saw Spider Woman.
Her thread had saved him. She had tied one end to a rock.
Then she dropped the other end to the ground.

8

The peaceful young man said thank you.
Then he climbed down the thread and ran home.
He told his family how Spider Woman had saved him.

9

Dictionary

Look at the picture. Read the word.
Write the word on the line.

Story Words

canyon	climb	cloth	family
_____	_____	_____	_____
magic	rock	spider	thread
_____	_____	_____	_____

Words to Know

beautiful	chased	enemy	hanging
helped	himself	peaceful	place
showed	tell	tied	young

I Read Closely

Read. Mark the sentence that goes with the picture.

○ The young man took a rest in that beautiful place.

○ He wanted to climb the tall rock.

○ Then she made her home at the top of Spider Rock.

○ He climbed up to the top of Spider Rock.

○ He was being chased by an enemy.

○ Spider Rock is a tall, tall rock in a canyon.

○ He told his family how Spider Woman had saved him.

○ She had tied one end to a rock.

I Read and Understand

Read and answer.

1. Spider Rock is ____.

   ○ magic

   ○ tall

2. The young man was ____.

   ○ peaceful

   ○ an enemy

3. Spider Woman dropped a ____ thread.

   ○ young

   ○ magic

4. The young man ____ up Spider Rock.

   ○ climbed

   ○ tied

5. The thread saved the young man from his ____.

   ○ enemy

   ○ canyon

I Tell the Story

Finish the pictures. Tell someone the story.

1 Draw the rock.

2 Draw the thread.

3 Draw the spider.

4 Draw the fire.

I told the story to _____.

I Read a Folk Tale

A folk tale is a made-up story.
Sometimes the characters are animals.
The story may be about a real place or thing.
It may have magic in it, too.

Setting

1. Where does the story take place?

_____

Magic

2. Which thing was magic?

_____

Problem

3. What problem did the young man have?

   ○ He needed to make beautiful cloth.

   ○ An enemy was chasing him.

4. How was the young man saved?

   ○ He ran home.

   ○ He climbed up Spider Rock.

I Can Write

Write the words to finish each sentence.

Word Box

| said thank you | the tall rock |
| by an enemy | saw Spider Woman |

1. A young man was chased _____.

2. He wanted to climb _____.

3. He turned around and _____.

4. The peaceful young man _____.

Write your own sentence. Tell where the story takes place.

5. _____

_____

_____